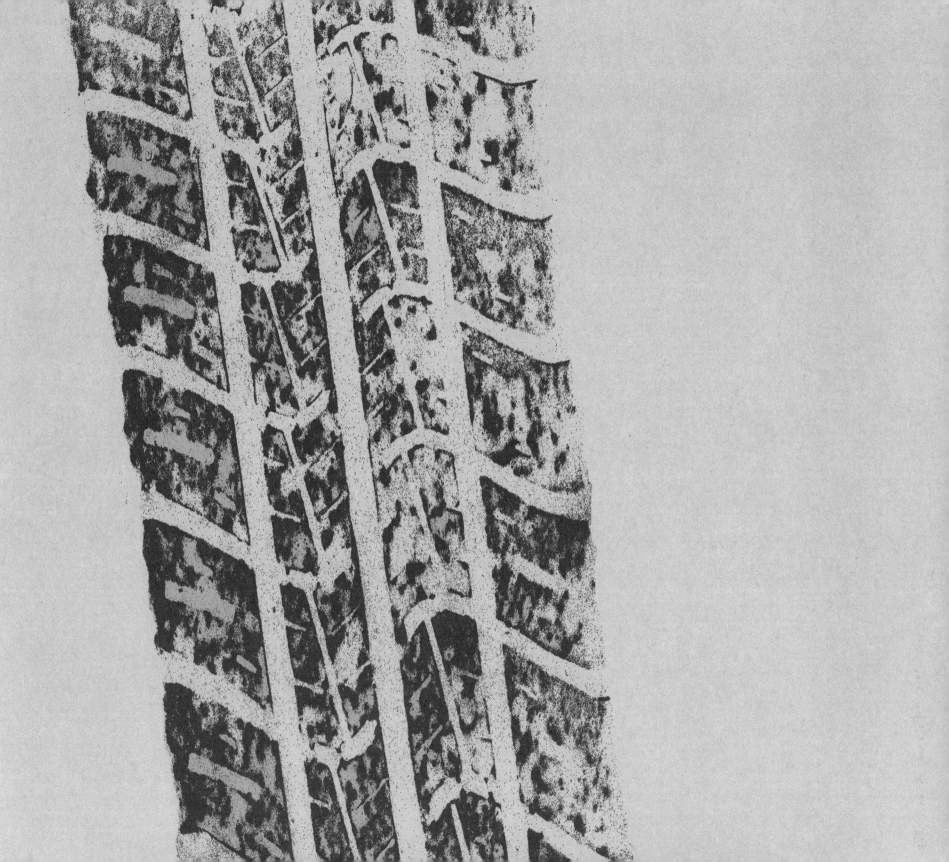

I DRIVE A
STREET SWEEPER

by **Sarah Bridges**

illustrated by **Amy Bailey Muehlenhardt**

PICTURE WINDOW BOOKS
Minneapolis, Minnesota

*Thanks to Bill Barnes of the City of Minneapolis
for all of the great stories. S.B.*

Editor: Jill Kalz
Designer: Jaime Martens
Page Production: Tracy Kaehler,
Zachary Trover, Brandie Shoemaker
Creative Director: Keith Griffin
Editorial Director: Carol Jones
The illustrations in this book were created digitally.

Picture Window Books
5115 Excelsior Boulevard
Suite 232
Minneapolis, MN 55416
877-845-8392
www.picturewindowbooks.com

Printed in the United States of America.

Library of Congress Cataloging-in-Publication Data
Bridges, Sarah.
I drive a street sweeper / by Sarah Bridges ;
illustrated by Amy Bailey Muehlenhardt.
p. cm. — (Working wheels)
Includes bibliographical references and index.
ISBN 1-4048-1608-9 (hardcover)
1. Street cleaning—Equipment and supplies—Juvenile
literature. 2. Street cleaning—Juvenile literature.
I. Muehlenhardt, Amy Bailey, 1974– ill. II. Title.
TD860.B75 2005
√628.4'6—dc22   2005023144

Pub 21⁰⁰ 5/25/06

Thanks to our advisers for their expertise, research, and advice:

Scott Dickinson, Marketing Manager
Schwarze Industries, Inc., Huntsville, Alabama

Susan Kesselring, M.A., Literacy Educator
Rosemount–Apple Valley–Eagan (Minnesota) School District

My name is Tami, and I drive a street sweeper. My job is to keep city streets clean. Each morning, I check my sweeper's brooms. I also check its fluids.

Street sweepers have three spinning brooms. There is one on each side of the vehicle and one in back.

It is a big step up to the cab. Inside are two seats and two steering wheels. I can drive the street sweeper from either seat.

Sometimes, street sweepers drive on the right side of the road. Other times, they drive on the left. Sweeper drivers can choose which seat and steering wheel gives them the better view of the curb.

Between the seats is a set
of levers. Some levers raise
or lower the brooms.

Other levers move the trash the street sweeper collects into the hopper.

Street sweeper drivers raise the brooms when going from one place to another. They lower the brooms to sweep the street.

My street sweeper sprays water on the road in front of the brooms. The water helps keep dust from blowing around while I sweep.

The trash collected by street sweepers must go into a special landfill because all kinds of things are mixed together. Trash sometimes includes poisonous chemicals or paint.

I lower the back broom. It makes a loud, swishing sound when it hits the ground. My sweeper follows the curb as I drive down the street.

The bristles on a street sweeper's broom feel a lot like the bristles on a household broom.

The broom sweeps dirt, sand, leaves, and trash onto a conveyor belt inside my street sweeper. The trash moves up the belt and falls into the hopper.

The conveyor belt looks a little like the belts that move groceries at a checkout counter. It has ridges that keep trash from sliding backward.

All kinds of trash are swept into my hopper. I see pop cans, cigarette butts, paper, and more. Sometimes I even see a tennis shoe!

Once in a while, a big piece of trash gets stuck inside the street sweeper. The driver then has to stop the vehicle and fix it.

Sometimes, street sweepers empty their trash into dump trucks. The dump trucks take the trash to a special landfill.

When my hopper is full, I go to a special landfill to empty it. I press a lever, and the hopper lifts into the air. Once it is high enough, I move the hopper to the side and dump out the trash.

At the end of the day, I drive my street sweeper to the garage and clean it. I spray the brooms and hopper with soap and water. Now it's ready to be put away for the night.

Street sweepers are repaired in special garages called sweeper shops.

STREET SWEEPER DIAGRAM

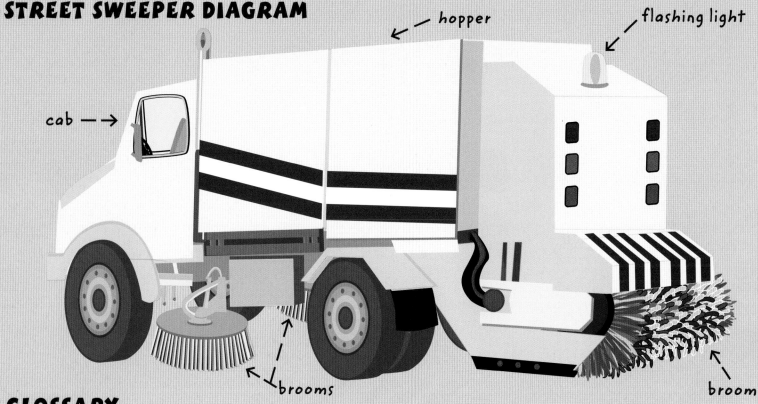

hopper

flashing light

cab →

brooms

broom

GLOSSARY

bristles—stiff hairs on a broom

cab—the front of a street sweeper where the driver sits

conveyor belt—a slow-moving belt that carries trash from a street sweeper's brooms to the hopper

curb—the raised edge of a street

fluids—liquids in the engine that make it run smoothly

hopper—a metal box at the top of a street sweeper that holds trash until it is dumped

landfill—a place where garbage is dumped and buried between layers of dirt

FUN FACTS

 The first motorized street sweepers appeared in the United States in the early 1900s. The sweeper had three wheels—one in back and two in front—and a hopper in front.

 Before starting work, street sweeper drivers turn on the flashing light on top of their vehicles. The light warns other drivers to stay back.

 Street sweepers do more than pick up trash. By keeping streets clean, sweepers don't leave much food for rodents or bugs to eat. Rodents and bugs can spread disease.

 In cold parts of the United States, street sweepers pick up a lot of salt and sand. These two things are put on roads in winter to keep cars from sliding around.

TO LEARN MORE

At the Library

Stickland, Paul. *Special Engines*. Columbus,
Ohio: Waterbird Books, 2004.

Sycamore, Beth. *Sweep!* New York:
Little Simon, 2003.

On the Web

FactHound offers a safe, fun way to find Internet sites
related to this book. All of the sites on FactHound
have been researched by our staff.

1. Visit www.facthound.com

2. Type in this special code
   for age-appropriate sites:
   1404816089

3. Click on the FETCH IT button.

Your trusty FactHound will fetch the best sites for you!

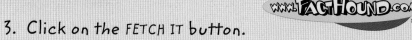

INDEX

LOOK FOR ALL OF THE BOOKS IN
THE WORKING WHEELS SERIES:

- I Drive a Backhoe
  1-4048-1604-6
- I Drive a Bulldozer
  1-4048-0613-X
- I Drive a Crane
  1-4048-1605-4
- I Drive a Dump Truck
  1-4048-0614-8

- I Drive a Fire Engine
  1-4048-1606-2
- I Drive a Freight Train
  1-4048-1607-0
- I Drive a Garbage Truck
  1-4048-0615-6
- I Drive an Ambulance
  1-4048-0618-0

- I Drive a Semitruck
  1-4048-0616-4
- I Drive a Snowplow
  1-4048-0617-2
- I Drive a Street Sweeper
  1-4048-1608-9
- I Drive a Tractor
  1-4048-1609-7